A Brief List of Everyone Who Died

Jacob Marx Rice

methuen | drama

LONDON · NEW YORK · OXFORD · NEW DELHI · SYDNEY

METHUEN DRAMA
Bloomsbury Publishing Plc
50 Bedford Square, London, WC1B 3DP, UK
1385 Broadway, New York, NY 10018, USA
29 Earlsfort Terrace, Dublin 2, Ireland

BLOOMSBURY, METHUEN DRAMA and the Methuen
Drama logo are trademarks of Bloomsbury Publishing Plc

First published in Great Britain 2023

Cover image: Flavier Fraser Cannon

Cover design: Solution Group

A catalogue record for this book is available from the British Library.

A catalog record for this book is available from the Library of Congress.

ISBN: PB: 978-1-3504-3009-9
ePDF: 978-1-3504-3010-5
eBook: 978-1-3504-3011-2

Series: Modern Plays

Typeset by Mark Heslington Ltd, Scarborough, North Yorkshire

To find out more about our authors and books visit
www.bloomsbury.com and sign up for our newsletters.

Amelia Campbell for Patch of Blue Theatre
in association with
Neil McPherson for the Finborough Theatre
presents

The world premiere

A Brief List of Everyone Who Died

by Jacob Marx Rice

First streamed online as part of #FinboroughFrontier:
Monday, 24 May 2021

First performance at the Finborough Theatre:
Tuesday, 16 May 2023

A Brief List of Everyone Who Died

by Jacob Marx Rice

Cast in order of appearance

Raul/Nurse	**Alejandro De Mesa**
Anne/Medical Resident/Lily	**Kathryn Akin**
Gracie/Grace/Graciela	**Vivia Font**
Jordan/Melaku	**Siphiwo Mahlentle**
Cass/Offstage Voice	**Amelia Campbell**

The approximate running time is 75 minutes.

There will be no interval.

Director	**Alex Howarth**
Set and Costume Designer	**Alice McNicholas**
Lighting and Video Designer	**Rachel Sampley**
Producer	**Amelia Campbell**
Assistant Director	**Anastasia Bunce**
Stage Manager	**Lucy Liquor**

Masks are optional, but recommended, except on Covid Safe Sunday matinees when they are mandatory.

Please turn your mobile phones off – the light they emit can be distracting.

Our patrons are respectfully reminded that, in this intimate theatre, any noise such as the rustling of programmes, talking or the ringing of mobile phones may distract the actors and your fellow audience members.

We regret there is no admittance or re-admittance to the auditorium whilst the performance is in progress.

Kathryn Akin | Anne/Medical Resident/Lily

Theatre includes: *Anyone Can Whistle* (Southwark Playhouse), *Death Takes a Holiday* (Charing Cross Theatre), *Next to Normal* (Tarragon Theatre, Toronto, Theatre Calgary and Citadel Theatre, Edmonton), *Calendar Girls* (Royal Alexandra Theatre, Toronto), *The Immigrant* (Toronto Centre for the Arts), *Carousel* (Savoy Theatre), *Gone with the Wind* (New London Theatre), *The Witches of Eastwick* (Theatre Royal Drury Lane), *Sunset Boulevard* (Adelphi Theatre), *Taboo* (New End Theatre), *Gypsy* (Dundee Rep), *Dona Flor and Her Two Husbands* (Lyric Hammersmith), *Smudge* (Ovalhouse), *The Typographer's Dream* (Pleasance Edinburgh), *Dorothy Fields Forever* (King's Head Theatre), *Trance* (White Bear Theatre), *The Wizard of Oz* (Bristol Old Vic), *Martin Guerre* (Leeds Playhouse and national tour for Cameron Mackintosh), *Celle-La/That Woman* (Traverse Theatre, Edinburgh, and Tramway, Glasgow), and principal roles in Canada's leading theatres including the Shaw Festival Theatre, the Stephenville Theatre Festival, Young People's Theatre, National Arts Centre and the Grand Theatre.

Film includes: *Barbie, Snow White* and *Mamma Mia! Here We Go Again*.

Television includes: *How (Not) to Kill Your Husband, Cambridge Spies, Aircrash Confidential* and *Street Legal*.

Radio includes: *Sunnyville, Afghanada, Peyton Place, On the Banks of Plum Creek, Bel Canto, Helpless* and *With Great Pleasure*.

Kathryn is also a very experienced voice artist.

Amelia Campbell | Cass/Offstage Voice

Trained at Actors Centre Australia.

Theatre includes: *MARS: An Interplanetary Cabaret*, *Playlist* (Seymour Centre), *The Sandpiper* (Old 505 Theatre, Sydney), *Chemistry* (Sydney Fringe Festival), *The Importance of Being Earnest* (National Institute of Dramatic Art), *Portia Coughlan*, *Hamlet*, *Children of the Sun* and *transience* (Actors Centre Australia) and *The Magician's Cabaret* (Jones Bay Wharf).

Film includes: *Out on a Limb*, *The Pool* and *She's Gone*.

Alejandro De Mesa | Raul/Nurse

Theatre includes: *La Bayadère* and *The Exterminating Angel* (Royal Opera House, Covent Garden), *Your Connection Is Not Private* (Coney), *Turmoil* (Courtyard Theatre) and *Dis Place* (Camden People's Theatre).

Film includes: *Pokémon Detective Pikachu* and *Snow White*.

Television includes: *The Coroner* and *Devs*.

Vivia Font | Gracie/Grace/Graciela

Theatre includes: *Play On!*, *Villa* (The Wild Project, New York City), *Recent Alien Abductions* (Walkerspace, New York City), *underneathmybed* (Rattlestick Playwrights Theatre, New York City), *Romeo and Juliet* (New York Classical Theatre, New York City), *The Art of Burning* (Huntington Theatre, Boston and Hartford Stage, Hartford), *The Sign in Sidney Brustein's Window*, *The Two Gentlemen of Verona*, *The Tenth Muse* (Oregon Shakespeare Festival),

Richard III, *As You Like It*, *Inherit the Wind*, *Six Degrees of Separation* (Old Globe Theatre, San Diego), *Mariela in the Desert*, *Map of Heaven* (Denver Center for the Performing Arts), *Native Gardens* (Merrimack Rep, Lowell) and *Mutual Philanthropy* (New Jersey Rep).

Film includes: *Love, Repeat* and *Sarbane's Oxley*.

Television includes: *Law & Order*, *FBI: Most Wanted*, *For Life* and *One Life to Live*.

Siphiwo Mahlentle | Jordan/Melaku

Trained at Arts Educational Schools, National Youth Theatre and Identity School of Acting.

Theatre includes: *All the Conversations We Haven't Had Yet*, *The Convert*, *Sucker Punch*, *Hamlet* (Arts Educational Schools) and *Scroogelicious* (Theatre Peckham).

Film includes: *They'll Love You*.

Jacob Marx Rice | Playwright

Productions at the Finborough Theatre include *Chemistry*.

Jacob's plays have been produced and developed in over a dozen cities on three continents at theatres including Eugene O'Neill Theatre Centre, Finborough Theatre in London, Actors Theatre of Louisville, Flea Theater in New York, Alex Theatre St Kilda in Melbourne and Atlantic Theater Stage 2. His play *Chemistry* was hailed by *The Guardian* as 'remarkable for its tender compassion' and by *The Stage* as 'A moving, insightful love story'. Jacob's plays won the Jean Kennedy Smith Playwriting Award from the Kennedy Center, an Ensemble Studio Theatre Sloan Commission and best of awards from fringe festivals around the world.

As a screenwriter, he won a Sloan Screenwriting Grant and the Faculty Award from NYU and is currently in development with Anonymous Content on his first feature.
www.jacobmarxrice.com

Alex Howarth | Director

Alex's productions at the Finborough Theatre include Jacob Marx Rice's *Chemistry*. He was recently named as one of 'Ten Stage Sensations to Watch Out For in 2023' by *The Guardian*.

Coming from the North West and a background of working in care, Alex is passionate about amplifying under-represented and northern voices. His play *Cassie and the Lights* (VAULT Festival, Adelaide Fringe and Underbelly) was based on a true story and interviews with children in the care system and is currently being developed for television. Nominated for the BBC Writersroom Popcorn Award and the SitUp Award for social change, as well as winning Best Theatre at Adelaide Fringe, it will transfer to 59E59 Theaters, Off Broadway, New York City this June.

He conceived, directed and co-wrote *We Live by the Sea* which has been seen internationally including 'Brits Off Broadway' at 59E59 Theaters, New York City, where it received Critic's Pick and Top Theatre of the Year in *The New York Times*; and at the Adelaide Fringe, where it won Best Theatre, Critic's Choice and the Grahame F. Smith Peace Foundation Award for promoting human rights. It was nominated for the Fringe First at the Edinburgh Festival, and Best Production and Best Ensemble at the OffWestEnd Awards.

He adapted and directed the world stage premiere of *What's Eating Gilbert Grape*, working alongside the film's writer, Oscar nominee Peter Hedges.

Recent theatre includes: *Medea* (Guildhall Amphitheatre) which won the Owl Schreame Award for Innovation in Classical Theatre, *The Greatest Hits of Lily and John* (The Other Palace), *Sweeney Todd* (Italia Conti), *Richard II* (Central School of Speech and Drama), the European premiere of *[title of show]* (Edinburgh Fringe), *The Memory Show* (Drayton Arms Theatre), *Back to Blackbrick* (Arts Theatre and tour), *Outlier: A New Opera* (Tête à Tête Opera), *Misterman* (New Wimbledon Theatre and Brockley Jack Theatre), *Two Sides* (Arcola Theatre), *Oh! You Pretty Things* (Southwark Playhouse), *The Fall* (Old Red Lion Theatre and tour), *Beans on Toast* (Theatre503 and tour), and *The Red Light* (Union Theatre).

Associate and Assistant Direction includes assisting Richard Eyre on *La Traviata* (Royal Opera House, Covent Garden) and Jeff Clarke on *Orpheus in the Underworld* (Buxton Opera House).

He leads research and development periods for new writing and has worked extensively in theatre with people with disabilities, having created performances with deafblind adults for the charity Sense, and recently co-created the one-man show *Strictly Lawrie* with disabled artist Lawrie Morris.

Alice McNicholas | Set and Costume Designer

Alice is a designer, specialising in costume for musical theatre and dance-based performance. She trained at the Royal Central School of Speech and Drama.

Set and Costume Design includes *Jack and the Beanstalk* (Applecart Arts), *Ally in Wonderland* (Ruined Theatre), *I'm F**king My Agent* (Golden Goose Theatre), *Tears of Laughter* (Tristan Bates Theatre) and *Our Teacher's a Troll* (Ruined Theatre).

Costume Design includes *Bell, Book and Candle* (Tabard Theatre), *Love Goddess: The Rita Hayworth Musical* (Cockpit Theatre), *A Critical Stage* (Tabard Theatre), *The Concrete Jungle Book* (Pleasance London), *Othello* (UK tour for Changeling Theatre), *The Importance of Being Earnest* (UK tour for Changeling Theatre), *Next Door's Baby* (Tabard Theatre), *Much Ado About Nothing* (summer tour for Bear in the Air Productions), *Cinderella* (Kenton Theatre), *Vinegar Tom* (Maltings Theatre), *Spring Awakening* (Embassy Theatre) and *La Calisto* (Cockpit Theatre).

Associate Costume Design includes Frantic Assembly's *Othello* (Lyric Hammersmith and UK tour), *Unfortunate* (Underbelly Earls Court) and *Candide* (Blackheath Halls Opera).

Rachel Sampley | Lighting and Video Designer

Rachel is a London-based video and lighting designer. Theatre includes: *Follow the Signs* (Soho Theatre), *Barriers* (National Theatre), *Opal Fruits* (Bristol Old Vic and Pleasance Edinburgh), *Cassie and the Lights* (Underbelly), *We Live by the Sea* (59E59 Theaters) and *Perfect Show for Rachel* (Barbican).

Amelia Campbell | Producer

Amelia Campbell is the Executive Producer for Patch of Blue Theatre, Founding Director of Wheels & Co Productions (Australia) and Artistic Director of the newly founded Sprig Rose Productions Ltd. (UK). Her producing work is inspired by collaborating with international writers. *A Brief List* is the second of Jacob Marx Rice's works that she has produced after producing *Chemistry* in Sydney in 2018.

Theatre includes: *Not Even God Can Save Us* (Actors Centre Australia), *Buried* (Old 505 Theatre), *Chemistry* (Sydney Fringe), *Wink* (KXT), *Leni and Joseph* (industry reading) and *Cassie and the Lights* (Underbelly).

She has also worked as Associate Producer on *Alice in Slasherland* (Old Fitz Theatre) and as First Assistant Director on *Her Own Music*, *The Casting Game* and *Soldiers*.

Anastasia Bunce | Assistant Director

Productions at the Finborough Theatre include directing *Darkie Armo Girl*, and assistant directing on *12:37* and *Not Quite Jerusalem*.

Trained in Theatre Directing at Mountview Academy of Theatre Arts. She is the Artistic Director of Patch Plays, a company devoted to staging new work that explores animal ethics and environmental sustainability.

Theatre includes OffWestEnd Award finalist *Meat Cute* (Vault Festival, shortly to be seen at the Gilded Balloon, Edinburgh).

Lucie Liquor | Stage Manager

Lucie has previously stage managed for multiple House of Burlesque shows including House of Burlesque Speakeasy (Sway Bar) and House of Burlesque Fresh (Royal Vauxhall Tavern). She also worked as a Production Intern for the House of Burlesque Politits at the Vaults Festival 2023.

Production Acknowledgements

Valma Briggs, The Campbell, Calvert & Desvaux de Marigny Families, Rita Dubovsky, Juliet's Quality Foods, Nicholina Kuner, Andrea Lopez, Paco Lozano, Grace Mackenzie, Deborah Marx, David Mendizábal, Michelle Orosz, Chip Rice, Maeliosa Stafford, Trish Wadley Productions, Ian Walton Photography, and all those who shared their stories and their lives to make this play possible.

FINBOROUGH
THEATRE

"Probably the most influential fringe theatre in the world." *Time Out*

"Not just a theatre, but a miracle." *Metro*

"The mighty little Finborough which, under Neil McPherson, continues to offer a mixture of neglected classics and new writing in a cannily curated mix." Lyn Gardner, *The Stage*

"The tiny but mighty Finborough" Ben Brantley, *The New York Times*

Founded in 1980, the multi-award-winning Finborough Theatre presents plays and music theatre, concentrated exclusively on vibrant new writing and unique rediscoveries from the 19th and 20th centuries, both in our 154-year-old home and online through our #FinboroughFrontier digital initiative.

Our programme is unique – we never present work that has been seen anywhere in London during the last 25 years. Behind the scenes, we continue to discover and develop a new generation of theatre makers.

Despite remaining completely unsubsidised, the Finborough Theatre has an unparalleled track record for attracting the finest talent who go on to become leading voices in British theatre. Under Artistic Director Neil McPherson, it has discovered some of the UK's most exciting new playwrights including Laura Wade, James Graham, Mike Bartlett, Jack Thorne, Nicholas de Jongh and Anders Lustgarten, and directors including Tamara Harvey, Robert Hastie, Blanche McIntyre, Kate Wasserberg and Sam Yates.

Artists working at the theatre in the 1980s included Clive Barker, Rory Bremner, Nica Burns, Kathy Burke, Ken Campbell, Jane Horrocks and Claire Dowie. In the 1990s, the Finborough Theatre first became known for new writing including Naomi Wallace's first play *The War Boys*, Rachel Weisz in David Farr's *Neville Southall's Washbag*, four plays by Anthony Neilson including *Penetrator* and *The Censor*, both of which transferred to the Royal Court Theatre, and new plays by Richard Bean, Lucinda Coxon, David Eldridge and Tony Marchant. New writing development included the premieres of modern classics such as Mark Ravenhill's *Shopping and F**king*,

Conor McPherson's *This Lime Tree Bower*, Naomi Wallace's *Slaughter City* and Martin McDonagh's *The Pillowman*.

Since 2000, new British plays have included Laura Wade's London debut *Young Emma*, commissioned for the Finborough Theatre, James Graham's *Albert's Boy* with Victor Spinetti, Sarah Grochala's *S27*, Athena Stevens' *Schism* which was nominated for an Olivier Award, and West End transfers for Joy Wilkinson's *Fair*, Nicholas de Jongh's *Plague Over England*, Jack Thorne's *Fanny and Faggot*, Neil McPherson's Olivier Award nominated *It Is Easy to Be Dead*, and Dawn King's *Foxfinder*.

UK premieres of foreign plays have included plays by Brad Fraser, Lanford Wilson, Larry Kramer, Tennessee Williams, Suzan-Lori Parks, Jordan Tannahill, the English premieres of two Scots-language classics by Robert McLellan, and West End transfers for Frank McGuinness' *Gates of Gold* with William Gaunt and John Bennett, and Craig Higginson's *Dream of the Dog* with Dame Janet Suzman.

Rediscoveries of neglected work – most commissioned by the Finborough Theatre – have included the first London revivals of Rolf Hochhuth's *Soldiers* and *The Representative*, both parts of Keith Dewhurst's *Lark Rise to Candleford*, Etta Jenks with Clarke Peters and Daniela Nardini, Noël Coward's first play *The Rat Trap*, Lennox Robinson's *Drama at Inish* with Celia Imrie and Paul O'Grady, and Emlyn Williams' *Accolade*, and John Van Druten's *London Wall* (both of which transferred to St James' Theatre), and J. B. Priestley's *Cornelius* which transferred to a sell-out Off Broadway run in New York City.

Music theatre has included the new (premieres from Craig Adams, Grant Olding, Charles Miller, Michael John LaChuisa, Adam Guettel, Andrew Lippa, Paul Scott Goodman, and Adam Gwon's *Ordinary Days* which transferred to the West End) and the old (the UK premiere of Rodgers and Hammerstein's *State Fair* which also transferred to the West End), and the acclaimed 'Celebrating British Music Theatre' series.

The Finborough Theatre won the 2020 London Pub Theatres Pub Theatre of the Year Award, The Stage Fringe Theatre of the Year Award in 2011, London Theatre Reviews' Empty Space Peter Brook Award in 2010 and 2012, swept the board with eight awards at the 2012 OffWestEnd Awards, and was nominated for an Olivier Award in 2017 and 2019. Artistic Director Neil McPherson was awarded the Critics' Circle Special Award for Services to Theatre in 2019. It is the only unsubsidised theatre ever to be awarded the Channel 4 Playwrights Scheme bursary eleven times.

www.finboroughtheatre.co.uk

The Finborough Theatre is a member of the Independent Theatre Council, the Society of Independent Theatres, Musical Theatre Network, The Friends of Brompton Cemetery and The Earl's Court Society, and supports #time4change's Mental Health Charter.

Supported by

The Theatres Trust Theatres Protection Fund Small Grants Programme, supported by The Linbury Trust

The Finborough Theatre receives no regular funding from the Royal Borough of Kensington and Chelsea.

Mailing
Email admin@finboroughtheatre.co.uk or give your details to our Box Office staff to join our free email list.

Playscripts
Many of the Finborough Theatre's plays have been published and are on sale from our website.

Local History
The Finborough Theatre's local history website is online at
www.earlscourtlocalhistory.co.uk

On Social Media

 www.facebook.com/FinboroughTheatre

 www.twitter.com/finborough

 www.instagram.com/finboroughtheatre

 www.youtube.com/user/finboroughtheatre

 https://www.tiktok.com/@finboroughtheatre

Friends
The Finborough Theatre is a registered charity. We receive no public funding, and rely solely on the support of our audiences. Please do consider supporting us by becoming a member of our Friends of the Finborough Theatre scheme. There are four categories of Friends, each offering a wide range of benefits.

Smoking is not permitted in the auditorium.
The videotaping or making of electronic or other audio and/or visual recordings or streams of this production is strictly prohibited.

In accordance with the requirements of the Royal Borough of Kensington and Chelsea:
1. The public may leave at the end of the performance by all doors and such doors must at that time be kept open.
2. All gangways, corridors, staircases and external passageways intended for exit shall be left entirely free from obstruction whether permanent or temporary.
3. Persons shall not be permitted to stand or sit in any of the gangways intercepting the seating or to sit in any of the other gangways.

A Brief List of Everyone Who Died

Characters

Gracie/Grace/Graciela, *female. Mixed race: Puerto Rican and Irish-American.*
Raul, *male. Puerto Rican. Graciela's father.*
Anne, *female. Irish-American. Graciela's mother.*
Jordan, *male. African-American. Graciela's childhood best friend.*
Cass, *female. Half Jewish, half goy. Graciela's girlfriend, then wife.*

Offstage Voice, *played by the same actor who plays Cass.*
Melaku, *male. Ethiopian. Graciela and Cass's son. Played by the same actor who plays Jordan.*
Medical Resident, *a resident at the hospital. Played by the same actor who plays Anne.*
Lily, *female. Melaku's daughter. Played by the same actor who plays Anne.*
Nurse, *male. Played by the same actor who plays Raul.*

A Note on Character Ages

This play takes place over the course of many decades, meaning the characters age significantly. The actors can be whatever age you think will be compelling, though I recommend casting everyone in their forties and letting the writing and acting define the ages.

Setting

A human life. Graciela is born in 1979.

Punctuation

Punctuation follows speech patterns over grammatical convention. Additionally, the following punctuation marks have the following specific meanings:

A dash (–) indicates an interruption by either the speaker themself or by a new speaker.
A slash (/) indicates the point of interruption if it is not at the end of the line.
An ellipse (. . .) indicates a slow trailing off, either on purpose or accidental.
A dash-ellipse (– . . .) signifies a sudden stop and then a silent continuation of thought.

Age 5

Raul *carefully places raisins on a bowl of farina as* **Anne** *waits for him to finish. The sound of Sunday morning cartoons in the background.*

Raul   She seemed fine, right?

Anne   Yes.

Raul   Too fine?

Anne *rolls her eyes.*

Anne   Are you done with your masterpiece?

Raul   One more thing.

He powders the farina with cinnamon. **Anne** *starts leaving.*

Raul   It's just weird. She didn't mention it last night. Or this morning. She's watching Garfield cartoons in there like everything is normal.

Anne   Normal is good.

Raul   But there's nothing normal about . . .

Anne   Of course there is. Death is the most normal thing in the world.

She exits to the living room. **Raul** *adds more raisins to the farina, then realises it's too many and takes a couple off.*

Gracie (*O/S*)   Breakfast!

Gracie *bounds into the kitchen.* **Anne** *follows.*

Raul   I made you a special breakfast today.

Gracie   Ice cream?

Raul   Even better.

He slides her the bowl of farina. This is not *better than ice cream.*

Raul   From your *abuelo*'s recipe. The best farina in Arecibo.

Gracie *eats.* **Raul** *and* **Anne** *watch. She doesn't notice.*

Raul   How are you feeling, *mija*?

Gracie   Do raisins grow on trees?

Raul   Raisins are tiny pieces of the moon that fly through space until –

Anne *nudges* **Raul**.

Anne   Raisins are dried grapes, Bobo. They grow on vines.

Gracie   Oh. That's boring.

Raul *gloats quietly.*

Gracie   The earth got hit by a space rock.

Annie   It did?

Gracie   Jordan said a space rock smashed all the dinosaurs a million bajillion years ago but I said he was lying and Ms. Chu said he was right and I shouldn't bite him.

Anne   Wait, you bit Jordan?

Gracie   No.

Anne   We've talked about biting, Gracie. It hurts people and you don't want to hurt people.

Gracie   Can I bite Buster? He's not people.

Anne *and* **Raul** *exchange a look.*

Gracie   Where is he?

Anne   Do you remember the conversation we had yesterday, Bobo? We were in the living room and we brought Buster in to say goodbye.

Gracie   Yesterday was too busy. I had to draw and play Lite-Brite.

Raul   *Mija*, you know how Buster's been feeling not so good? And he had to wear that funny cone?

Gracie   Ice-cream cone!

Raul   Exactly. He wore an ice-cream cone because he was sick. You remember that?

Gracie *nods*.

Raul   Well, we . . . So, there's this farm.

Anne   Raul. (*To* **Gracie**.) Buster passed away.

Gracie   What's that?

Anne   It means that Buster is dead now.

Gracie   When does he come back?

Raul   What?

Anne   Buster is gone, Bobo. For always.

Gracie   No.

Raul   It's gonna be okay, *mija*.

Gracie   No. He can't go. I didn't say goodbye.

Anne   You did, remember? Yesterday in the living room.

Gracie   I didn't say goodbye!

Anne   We were in the living room and Buster was –

Gracie   Give me back my doggy!

Pause. They don't know what to say.

Gracie   I hate you.

Raul   Graciela, don't say things like that.

Gracie   I hate you. I hate you. You made my doggy dead.

Anne   That's not what happened, Bobo.

Gracie   Give me back my doggy! Give me back my doggy!

Pause. They wait patiently. **Gracie** *whimpers*.

Gracie   I didn't even say goodbye.

Age 8

Jordan *lies on the ground with his hands crossed over his chest.*
Gracie *walks towards him holding plastic flowers. She sings a*
wordless song and places the flowers on **Jordan**, *who keeps his eyes*
closed.

Jordan   Now what?

Gracie   Uhh . . . A man gives a speech in a funny robe.

Jordan   I can give a speech!

Gracie   No, you're the funeral.

Jordan   That's not fair. This game is dumb.

Gracie   You're dumb!

Jordan (*hurt*)   Am not.

Gracie   I know. You're the smartest kid in our class.

Jordan   Smarter than Benjie?

Gracie   Okay, second. I'm like . . . thirty.

Jordan   We only have twenty-eight.

Gracie   Oh, yeah.

Jordan   You're smart when you pay attention.

Gracie   Mrs. Mackintosh said I have ADD. Which doesn't
make sense cuz I'm not even good at math. She wanted me
to eat pills, but Daddy called it "gringo bullshit."

Jordan   They wanted you to eat poop pills?

Gracie   Adults are gross. You can give the speech. But we
have to find you a robe.

Jordan   Let's watch *Land Before Time*!

Gracie   Not until after. You can't go to heaven without a
funeral.

Jordan   My dad says heaven's not real.

Gracie Of course heaven is real. That's where my doggy is.

Jordan I thought Bella was in the kitchen.

Gracie My real doggy. He died and my parents didn't even let me say goodbye.

Jordan Why?

Gracie People are bad sometimes. I bet my *abuelo* and Buster play fetch all the time in heaven, even though my *abuelo* wasn't very good at throwing.

Jordan What's an *abuelo*?

Gracie He was my dad's dad. He got funeraled for real.

Jordan Whoa, your dad has a dad?

Gracie Doesn't your dad have a dad?

Jordan I don't think so. He just has my grandpa.

Gracie I don't like my grandpa. My *abuelo* was way better, even though I didn't know him too good cuz he lived in Arecibo and he only spoke Spanish.

Jordan You don't speak Spanish? But I thought you were Hispanish?

Gracie My dad never taught me cuz learning two languages would make it hard to astimulate.

Jordan Weird.

Gracie You're weird. Why don't you speak, like, African or something?

Jordan Cuz of slavery.

Gracie What's slavery?

Jordan People made other people work for free and then hit them.

Gracie That sucks.

Jordan   Yeah. Do you think they have dinosaurs in heaven?

Gracie   Maybe.

Jordan   That's so cool. I'm gonna make friends with a diplodocus.

Gracie   What's a dipocalypse?

Jordan   Diplodocus. It's the best dinosaur ever. We could all be friends up in heaven. You and me and Buster and the Diplodocus.

Gracie   I don't wanna go to heaven. I like it here too much.

Jordan   But if everyone else goes to heaven, won't you be lonely?

Grace *considers*.

Gracie   No one can go to heaven!

Jordan   No one at all?

Gracie   No one I like. My grandpa can go.

Raul (*O/S*)   Gracie. Jordan. Time for lunch.

Gracie   If nobody I like ever goes to heaven, then I won't ever have to be sad.

Jordan   But I'm still sad sometimes even though I don't know anyone in heaven.

Gracie   You know lots of dinosaurs. Maybe you're sad because they're in heaven.

Jordan   That makes sense.

Gracie   Ooh! We can unfuneral the depossumist and bring it back to earth!

Jordan   I'd never be sad with a diplodocus best friend.

Gracie   Umm, I'm your best friend.

Jordan   Oh, yeah. The diplodocus can be my second-best friend.

Raul *enters.*

Raul   Come on. I made fish sticks.

Jordan   Can we watch *Land Before Time* after lunch?

Raul   Again? You're gonna wear out the tape.

Gracie   Dinosaurs make Jordan not feel sad.

Raul   I'll set up the VCR.

Jordan   Thanks, Mr. Ruiz. I'm sorry about your dad.

Raul   That's . . . Thank you, Jordan. That's very sweet of you.

Age 13

Gracie *sits at the dining table doing homework.* **Anne** *cooks.*

Anne   Is Jordan still coming over tonight?

Gracie (*aggressively*)   No.

Anne   Okay? (*Pause.*) Is something wrong?

Gracie   He's a boy.

Anne   Ahh.

Gracie   Don't 'ahh' like you get it.

Anne   Why don't you try explaining to me?

A withering eye roll from **Gracie**.

Anne   If I don't understand, that'll prove you're superior.

Pause as **Gracie** *considers this.*

Gracie   He asked me to the dance.

Anne   Winter formal?

Gracie   What other dance?

Anne   You know, sometimes friendship can slowly turn into something –

Gracie   Can you stop being such a mom?

Anne   What do you want me to say, Bobo?

Gracie   That Jordan's a shithead.

Anne   Language, Graciela.

Gracie   He asked me in front of everybody.

Anne   I'm sure he didn't do it to upset you. Sometimes this happens. People get their wires crossed about what they mean to each other.

Gracie   Then why not, like, talk to me instead of doing some big thing in front of everybody?

Annie   Maybe he thought you'd find it romantic?

Gracie   Because he's dumb.

Anne   You two will figure it out.

Gracie   How do you know?

Anne   I wasn't always a mom. When I was your age, I was a lot like Jordan.

Gracie   A nerd?

Anne   No. Well, that too. But I had a crush on my best friend.

Gracie   You were best friends with Dad?

Anne   No.

Gracie   Eww.

Anne   His name was Buddy.

Gracie   That's a dog's name.

Anne   His real name was Richard. He went to the boys' school across the street and we always walked home together. I liked him so much I thought parts of my body would fall out.

Gracie   Which parts?

Anne   Every night I prayed an entire rosary that Buddy would ask me to the Spring Fling. And then I had to confess to Father Joseph for misusing my rosary.

Gracie   Did Buddy ask you?

Anne   He asked Cynthia Mayfield. So, I kicked him in the shin.

Gracie   Mom!

Anne   Where do you think you get your stinking attitude?

Gracie   That's so cool.

Anne   We actually ended up dating in high school. But it didn't work out.

Gracie   Cuz he wasn't Dad.

Anne   Sure.

Pause.

Gracie   What if I never have a Buddy?

Anne   It's not a very common nickname anymore.

Gracie   I mean . . . I've never liked a guy enough to kick him in the shin.

Anne   You're young.

Gracie   I'm thirteen.

Anne   You'll find the young man worth kicking in the shin. You'll probably find several.

Gracie   Eww.

Anne   And when you're ready, you'll find a pair of shins you want to make a life with. But sometimes there will be boys you don't want to kick in the shin. And that doesn't make them bad people.

Gracie   He embarrassed me.

Anne   And you saying no in front of all your friends, do you think that might be embarrassing for him too?

Pause.

Anne   You never have to kick anyone in the shin if you don't want to. But to put your deepest feelings out there for someone to shoot down, that's pretty hard too maybe.

Gracie   I guess.

Anne   And I bet he wishes he could talk to his best friend about it.

Gracie   I'm not his best friend. Benjie is.

Anne   Graciela . . .

Gracie   Fine. He can come for dinner.

The phone rings.

Anne   That's very mature of you.

Gracie   Wait, Buddy's real name is Richard? And he went to school across the street? Did you date Uncle Richard?

The phone rings again. **Anne** *laughs and walks over to it.*

Annie   He's not actually your uncle.

Gracie   He's got a boat!

Anne *picks up the phone.*

Anne   Hello?

Her tone changes.

Anne   Greg? . . . Greg, slow down, you're not making any sense . . . What do you . . . When? . . . No, that's . . . Greg. No, Greg. She can't be . . .

A long pause.

Anne   I can call them . . . It's fine. I'll just . . . Yeah. I love you too.

She hangs up. She sits down on the ground, involuntarily.

Anne   Mommy.

Gracie *watches, unsure how to help.*

Age 18

Raul *enters with a phone. He paces and frets. He pushes numbers on the phone.*

A beeper sound. **Grace** *enters and walks over to a phone on a table. She's talking to someone offstage.*

Grace   I press nine to call out, right?

Offstage Voice   Call later. It's your turn.

She puts the beeper away and exits.

Grace (*O/S*)   Alright. I'd fuck Achilles, marry Hector, and kill Paris.

Raul *redials. The pager goes off again.*

Grace (*O/S*)   Lisa's up. The apple question. Athena, Aphrodite, and Hera. Assuming it wouldn't start a war.

Raul *redials. The pager goes off again.*

Grace (*O/S*)   Sorry, my dad's been super-clingy. He's empty nesting.

Offstage Voice (*O/S*)   Ignore him, Grace. That's what parents are for.

Grace (*O/S*)   I'll just make sure he doesn't think I've been murdered.

She enters and dials the phone. **Raul** *picks up immediately.*

Grace   You know, pagers keep messages. You don't have to keep paging.

Raul   I know. I just . . . How's school?

Grace   Studying the *Iliad*. What's the emergency?

Raul   We went to the vet today. Just now. Bella's arthritis is getting worse. There's nothing they can do. They said we should . . . That the compassionate thing would be . . .

Grace   To put her down.

Raul   Your mom and I are happy to pay for your ticket home. However long you need.

Grace   That's really sweet, Dad, but I'm about to go into midterms and things are . . . Did I tell you I joined the newspaper?

Raul   That's wonderful, *mija*. Will you send me your articles? I'll put them on the fridge.

Grace   Sure. But with Bella, you guys should put her down without me.

Raul   Are you serious? What about Buster?

Grace   What about him?

Raul   You told everyone we killed your dog.

Grace   I was five. I probably forgot I said goodbye.

Raul   You did. You did forget. God, we tried everything. Ice cream. *Quesitos*. Power Rangers.

Grace   Wait, I got that Power Rangers play-set because you killed my dog?

Raul   *No lo matamos!*

Grace   I was joking, Dad. Wow, I really traumatized you.

Raul   No, it was . . . You were very passionate.

Grace   I'm never having kids.

Raul   Okay.

Grace   Is this one of those okays where you think I'm wrong but you don't want to argue?

Raul   You are wrong. And I don't want to argue.

Grace   I should get back to studying.

Raul   You sure you won't hold this against us for a decade?

Grace   I make no promises.

Raul   I love you, *mija*.

Grace   You too. And hug Bella for me. She's a good dog.

Raul   She is. She is a good, good dog.

Age 23

Grace *and* **Jordan** *stand together in formal wear.*

Jordan   I didn't know you owned dresses.

Grace   I'm sophisticated now.

He gives her the side eye.

Grace   I borrowed it from a friend.

Jordan   A friend or a *friend*?

She ignores the question.

Grace   It looks good.

Grace   If you ask me to winter formal, I swear to God . . .

Jordan   You're safe.

Grace   Good. Lucy doesn't need more reasons to be a dick to me.

Jordan   She's really sweet once you get past . . .

Grace   Her personality?

Jordan   Gracie.

Grace   It's Grace now. Gracie is so last millennium.

Jordan   I'll call you a mature name when you act like a mature person.

Grace   That's hopeless.

Jordan   I know, Gracie.

Grace   Do you know how Pete . . .?

Jordan   Epileptic fit. He had a seizure and hit his head against the concrete. It was that fast.

Pause.

Grace   It's weird. I sorta figured people were immortal until at least forty.

Jordan   There's evidence against that everywhere.

Grace   I'm good at ignoring evidence.

Jordan   Won't that make you a bad lawyer?

Grace   Arguably, it'll make me a better lawyer.

Jordan   Remember when you decided nobody you loved was ever gonna die?

Grace   Why do you think you're still here?

An awkward pause.

Grace   I found out about Pete by email. I thought it was some sick prank. Death should come by raven or something. Not a Yahoo inbox. It was like, Editors meeting moved to Saturday, Pete's dead, Hawt XX Nudes.

Jordan   Editors meeting? You got the Law Review thingy?

Grace   I had to stab a couple people, but they deserved it.

Slight pause.

Grace   You should come visit. I have a futon, kinda. And it would be nice to see you for more than just weddings and funerals.

Jordan   I don't know . . .

Grace   Is this about the Towers?

Jordan   If there was an attack . . .

Grace   Al-Qaeda is not attacking Brooklyn.

Jordan   No one thought they were attacking Manhattan.

Grace   What do you even care? You're clearly not afraid of death.

Jordan   Ouch.

Grace   I didn't mean it like that.

Jordan   You kinda did.

Grace   Sorry.

Jordan   You can always come home to visit.

Grace   Last time I was here, you were too busy to text me back.

Jordan   I wasn't busy.

Pause.

Jordan   They don't let you check your phone in the psych ward.

Grace   You were back in the psych ward and you didn't tell me?

Jordan   I meant to. But my dad was constantly hovering and Lucy . . .

Grace   Lucy what?

Jordan   She was crying. A lot.

Grace   Why was she crying if you're the one with depression?

Jordan   We broke up. I mean, that's not why she was crying. She was crying because I swallowed a bottle of codeine and then we broke up and then she was probably crying cuz we broke up but I don't know for sure.

Grace   When you say, "we broke up," do you mean she dumped you for being depressed cuz she's a shallow bitch?

Jordan   I thought you weren't using that word anymore?

Grace   Some bitch dumping my best friend is more important than sexism.

Jordan   That's not really true.

Grace   Fine. But she's still garbage. Non-gender-specific garbage.

Jordan   You have no idea what it's like to date someone with depression.

Grace   I know you don't abandon people who need you.

Jordan   She came home from yoga to find me delirious and covered in vomit. She was traumatized.

Grace   And the solution was leaving you to handle it alone?

Jordan   She has her own shit to deal with. Everybody does. Even you.

Grace   Not fair. You didn't tell me.

Jordan   What would you have done? Quit law school and fly back to take care of me?

Grace   I'm soothing as fuck. We could watch *Land Before Time*.

Pause.

Jordan   I'm doing a lot better now.

Grace   Because you don't have to put up with Lucy.

He smiles.

Grace   It's nice. Seeing you. Even if it's for . . .

Jordan   Yeah.

Pause.

Grace   The last time I saw Pete was Catalina's graduation party.

Jordan   Before or after you puked your guts out?

Grace   During.

Jordan   Woof.

Grace   If he came to New York, I would've made an excuse about being busy and recommended MoMA. It's like, I wouldn't give him an hour for lunch if he were alive, but I'm taking three days off work to see his corpse.

Jordan   It's a closed casket.

Grace   To see the box holding his corpse. Even worse.

Jordan   You didn't have to come.

Grace   I think I did. Losing someone my age. Knowing it's possible to just . . . It feels like there's this threat I never even thought to worry about. Like when you work out after a long break and you have sore muscles in places you didn't know had muscles.

Jordan   I haven't done a real workout in years.

Grace   It's supposed to be good for depression.

Jordan   Thanks, doc.

Grace   Please don't make me go to one of these for you.

Jordan   It's not about you, Gracie.

Grace   I know, but –

Jordan   It's not about you.

Long pause.

Jordan   I'm doing a lot better.

Age 27

Graciela *and* **Cass** *pack suitcases.*

Cass   This is not how I imagined meeting your parents.

Graciela   This was always the plan. I was just waiting for the old man to croak.

Cass   Show some respect. He was your grandfather. His genetic code is a quarter of yours.

Graciela   No wonder I'm a quarter asshole.

Cass   Gratzi!

Pause.

Cass   Maybe we should wait. I could meet them another time. A happy time.

Graciela   Sure. Let's go for Thanksgiving.

Cass   Not fair.

Graciela   It's not fair to abandon your girlfriend for the holidays.

Cass   Holidays are different for us. You have your whole extended family.

Graciela   I hate my extended family.

Cass   You don't hate them. You like the idea of hating them.

Graciela   Can't I do both?

Cass   When I go home, it's just me and my brother and my dad. If I'm not there, that's the saddest Thanksgiving ever.

Graciela   It's fine. You don't love me enough to ruin Thanksgiving.

Cass   What about Easter?

Graciela   Easter means Easter mass.

Cass   I thought your family wasn't that religious?

Graciela   Once the Catholic church gets its claws in you . . .

Cass   What about Flag Day?

Graciela   This isn't about the funeral, is it? You're afraid they won't like you.

Cass   Of course they won't like the gringa defiling their daughter.

Graciela   My mom is Irish.

Cass   Great, more Catholics.

Graciela   They support gay marriage. They protested against SB 1250.

Cass   It's easy to be okay with things in the abstract. How many gay people do your parents actually know?

Graciela   We had a neighbour growing up who was either gay or really into lawn gnomes.

Cass   Bringing home a woman is . . . My dad is as accepting as they come, but the first time I brought a girl to meet him, he tried to bond by chopping wood.

Graciela   What? Why?

Cass   She wore a lot of flannel . . .

Graciela   Wow.

Cass   Imagine it. A nebbishy Jew and a Brooklyn scene queen trying to chop down a tree.

Graciela   My parents are gonna love you. And if they don't, I'll kick their asses.

Cass   My warrior princess.

They keep getting ready.

Cass   What was he like? Your grandpa.

Graciela   Think like the Lucky Charms leprechaun but taller and meaner and completely different in every way.

Cass   Bad jokes won't protect you from having feelings.

Graciela   Fuck you, my jokes are great.

Pause. **Cass** *waits patiently.*

Graciela   He was a grandpa. Not a particularly good grandpa. Or a good father as far as I could tell. Definitely a terrible husband. He worked in smelting. Or not actually smelting. Something in management for a steel company, but I told my third-grade class it was smelting and my mom said it wasn't smelting, so I told her she wasn't the boss of me and I would say smelting if I wanted to say smelting.

Cass   This story sounds like an excuse to repeat the word smelting.

Graciela   He had the hardness you imagine smelters have. Whatever smelting is. At holidays, he would sit on the couch with his *Wall Street Journal* and a glass of Jameson so he didn't have to talk to people. I once leaned back in my chair, when I was like eight or nine, and he threw a book at my head.

Cass   There must be one good memory.

Graciela   Besides smelting?

Pause.

Graciela   He . . . He'd give me chocolate.

Cass   That's something.

Graciela Irish chocolate. Made with Guinness and potatoes and the blood of Protestants. If I didn't break anything for a whole day, I could pick a single piece from this little wooden box. It had a picture of Saint Christopher on it, which is weird since this was after Vatican II. I guess he figured his guilty pleasure could be protected by a decanonized saint. I barely ever made it through a day without breaking something, but when I did, we'd sit on his bed and eat our chocolate together. Sometimes, he'd even give me a second piece.

Cass See, he was nice.

Graciela I think he wanted to be. You could feel it, even when I was little, that he was trying not to be so . . . He came here when he was seven, at the height of the Depression. He got called a mick every day. Kids would spit in his lunch and he ate it anyway because they were too poor to throw out food. That kind of life, it doesn't exactly make someone cozy.

Cass My grandparents were kinda like that. My mom's parents. My grandpa nearly died in the Pacific. And my grandma farmed for sixty years, four of those on her own with a husband half a world away, the rest with a husband whose leg couldn't bend from the shrapnel. There's a picture of her, pregnant, one of my uncles, three years old, clutching at her knees, and this blimp of a pregnant woman is digging a ditch.

Graciela We don't have challenges like that. World Wars. Crossing oceans. Starvation. The kind of experiences that show you who you are. The worst thing I've faced was my dog dying.

Cass They fought so we wouldn't have to. So we could complain about not being allowed to tilt back in chairs.

Graciela He must have thought I was such a brat.

Age 30

Graciela *enters, staring at her phone. When she sends [texts], they appear onstage.*

Graciela   [*Yo, I'm coming home for a cousin's memorial. Let's grab drunch!*]

Graciela [**lunch*]

Graciela   [*What does it say about my life that my phone autocorrects lunch to drunch?*]

Jordan *enters, also typing on his phone.*

Jordan   [*Sorry about your cousin. Was it Vanessa?*]

Graciela   [*Thanks. No. Some second cousin I met twice. But my family doesn't miss funerals, so . . .*]

Graciela   [*Vanessa just had a kid. She looks terrible.*]

Jordan   [*When are you back?*]

Graciela   [*14th–19th*]

Jordan   [*Yesterday?*]

Graciela   [*September. There's Dominicans on his mom's side and visa shit takes forever.*]

Graciela   [*Will you be around?*]

Days pass.

Graciela   [*?*]

Graciela   [*You free to hang when I'm home?*]

Jordan   [*Sure. I've got no plans.*]

Graciela   [*Great! Lunch on the 15th.*]

Jordan   [*Kk*]

Days pass.

Graciela   [*If Cass and I adopt a kid, would you be the godfather?*]

Graciela   [*Not in a religious way.*]

Graciela   [*Or an Italian gangster way.*]

Graciela   [*Though you would look pretty cool with a machine gun and a pile of cocaine.*]

Graciela   [*Or is that* Goodfellas*?*]

Graciela   [*I looked it up. Apparently, it's* Scarface.]

Graciela   [*Hello?*]

Jordan   [*You're adopting?*]

Graciela   [*We're fighting about it.*]

Graciela [**thinking*]

Graciela   [*So? Horse head in a bed?*]

Jordan   [*I don't think I'd be a good godfather.*]

She calls.

Graciela   I know the title is silly, but we're adopting from Ethiopia and I want him to have someone who can teach him the stuff my white-ass wife and I won't think of.

Jordan   I can show him the secret handshake without being his godfather.

Graciela   It's not like we're baptizing him. You just have to take him to the zoo when Cass and I want to have sex in the kitchen.

Slight pause.

Graciela   Please. If you're his godfather, it makes us, like, god siblings or something.

Jordan   Wouldn't it make us god married?

Graciela   I want you to be part of my family.

Pause.

Jordan   Fine.

Graciela   Such a pushover.

Jordan   Yeah.

Graciela   How are you doing? With all the . . .

Jordan   Better.

Graciela   Really?

Jordan   Are you seriously gonna adopt a kid? That's intense.

Graciela   The word you're looking for is terrifying.

Jordan   You'll be alright.

Graciela   Now that we've got the perfect godfather.

Jordan   Yeah.

Graciela   "Say hello to my little friend."

Jordan   Not *The Godfather*.

Graciela   Dammit. Love you.

Jordan   You too.

Days pass.

Graciela   [*A co-worker said Stegosaurus couldn't fight a T-Rex cuz they're from a different age or something. Truth?*]

A day passes. She calls.

Graciela   I text you for dinosaur knowledge and you ghost me? Seriously?

Jordan   [*Missed your call. Your co-worker is right.*]

Jordan   [*Stegosaurus are late Jurassic. T-Rex are Cretaceous.*]

Jordan   [*It's 70 million years between.*]

Graciela   [*Bullshit. They're both in* Land Before Time.]

Graciela   [*Why did you make me watch that movie six thousand times if it wasn't even accurate?*]

Days pass.

Graciela   [*We're still on for lunch in two weeks, right?*]

Jordan   [*Sure.*]

Graciela   [*You could sound more excited.*]

Jordan   [*Sure!*]

Days pass.

Graciela   [*Dropped that shit about Cretaceous and Jurassic in a meeting. They think I'm brilliant!*]

Days pass.

Graciela   [*Can we go to Harry's? I'm craving hoagies.*]

Graciela   [*Ooh, and Jed's Snack Shack for dessert.*]

Days pass.

Jordan   [*I'm sorry.*]

Jordan *walks offstage.*

Graciela   [*If you have to move lunch it's fine.*]

Graciela   [*Dude, your text freaked me out.*]

She calls.

Graciela   Hey, man, you can't send a random sorry text. Call me.

Graciela   [*Left you a message. Call me.*]

She calls.

Graciela   Seriously, dude, pick up.

Graciela   [*Call me.*]

The phone rings.

Graciela   Jordan? Thank – Oh, hi, Mrs. Cooper.

She listens. Her face drops.

Graciela   What? No, we had plans. We were getting lunch in a week. No. Mrs. Cooper. No. Please. Please. Please.

Age 37

Graciela *sits, working.* **Melaku** *enters with a fishbowl holding a single dead fish.*

Melaku   Eema, I think he's dead.

Graciela *stares at* **Melaku** *as if she doesn't recognize him.*

Melaku   See? He's floating silly.

He notices her lack of response.

Melaku   Eema?

Graciela   How do you . . . How do you know about death, Laku?

Melaku   Madison's uncle died last year. She missed school for the funeral. Can we funeral Phillip?

Graciela (*calling offstage*)   Cass.

Melaku   Mommy's in her office.

Graciela (*yelling*)   Cass!

Casss (*O/S*)   You alright?

Graciela   Can you please come to the kitchen?

Melaku   What do you do at funerals? Is there dancing? I like dancing.

Cass *enters.*

Cass   What's up?

Melaku   Phillip's floating funny cuz he died.

Cass   That's true. Fish, when they're not alive anymore, they float.

Melaku   Why?

Cass   Well, because they get lighter.

Melaku   Why?

Cass Because . . . I don't know, Laku. That's a good question.

Melaku Can we ask the Google?

Cass Sure.

Melaku Maybe they're trying to float up to heaven.

Graciela (*to herself*)   With the diplodocus.

Melaku What's a dipocalypse?

Graciela *doesn't know what to say. She stares off into the distance.*

Melaku Is Eema okay?

Cass She's just sad about Phillip.

Melaku Why?

Cass Sometimes people get sad when things die.

Melaku Why?

Cass Because losing things we care about can feel like losing a part of ourselves.

Melaku Why?

Cass Maybe you should draw a picture. In honor of Phillip.

Melaku I'll draw a rocket ship. Phillip loved rocket ships.

Cass You could draw a picture of him driving a rocket ship.

Melaku Dead fish can't drive rocket ships, Mommy.

Cass Why don't you go get your crayons?

Melaku Can Eema help? She draws the best fire part.

Cass Of course. You get started and Eema will help in a minute. I put the crayons by your box.

Melaku *leaves. A long pause.* **Graciela** *struggles with what to say.*

Graciela He looks just like Jordan did, when he was little. Standing there, talking about . . .

Cass   I know.

Graciela   I have to go.

Cass   What?

Graciela   I need a, a walk or something.

Cass   A child's first experience of death shapes how they approach it for the rest of their life. You need to be help him understand that it's okay.

Graciela   I can't.

Cass   Yes, you can. After Melaku goes to bed, you can have all the feelings you want. We can talk about Jordan. Anything. But until then, we're parents, not humans.

Pause.

Melaku (*O/S*)   I got crayons, Eema.

Pause.

Graciela   Coming!

Age 40

Raul *sits in a chair. He stands up as* **Melaku**, **Graciela**, *and* **Cass** *enter.* **Melaku** *runs and hugs* **Raul**.

Melaku   Abbo!

Raul   Oof. Look how tall you are, *mijo*.

Melaku   Eema says I'm a beanpole.

Raul   *Flaccito*. That means skinny boy.

Graciela   Him you'll teach Spanish?

Raul   I taught you Spanish.

Graciela   No, you didn't.

Raul   Oh right. But it was for your own good.

Graciela   You'd make a good lawyer. I didn't do it and if I did, I was right.

Raul   How sharper than a serpent's tooth to have a thankless child.

Melaku   How's Grandma?

Raul   She's doing much better, *mijo*.

Raul *and* **Graciela** *share a series of looks.*

Raul   Come on. Let's go get fro-yo.

Melaku *and* **Raul** *exit.* **Graciela** *starts to go in but stops.*

Cass   You've got this.

Graciela   She's not allowed to die.

Cass   Gratzi.

Graciela   She's not fucking allowed.

A long pause, then **Graciela** *enters the room.* **Cass** *waits outside in the hall.*

Anne   Hey, Bobo.

Graciela   How are you feeling?

Anne   I'm alright.

Graciela   How are you really feeling?

Pause.

Graciela   I think you should do it.

Anne   Your father told you about the procedure?

Graciela   The parts he could remember.

Anne   Did he tell you the chances of it working?

Graciela   I know they're not great, but –

Anne   Fifteen percent.

Graciela   We can't give up.

Anne   I'm not giving up. I'm making a choice.

Graciela   Mom.

Anne   Death is natural.

Graciela   Natural doesn't mean good. Hurricanes are natural. Hemorrhoids are natural.

Anne   I don't want to waste the rest of my life trying not to die. This way I can go out on my terms, surrounded by family.

Graciela   What about Laku? Don't you want to see him graduate in June?

Anne   They graduate from elementary school?

Graciela   There's a ceremony and everything. You can't miss that.

Anne   Graciela.

Graciela   No, you . . . I decided. Don't you remember? No one can die.

Anne   We don't get to decide that.

Graciela   At least try. For me.

Anne   I don't want your last memory of me to be hooked up to some terrifying machine.

Graciela   I don't care about the machine.

Anne   My death. My rules. This is not your call, Bobo.

Graciela   Then what? What do I . . .?

Anne   Do you remember when we lost Buster?

Graciela   Oh my God, I get it. I was an evil child.

Anne   You were a magnificent child. You were just . . . passionate.

Graciela   You and Dad love that euphemism.

Anne   Whatever happens. I want you to have this memory. Don't forget we said goodbye.

Graciela   Please.

Anne   The day you were born, I looked down at you in my arms and thought, 'How is it possible I can love something so ugly so much.' But I did. I loved watching you slam headfirst into every obstacle. I loved helping you build a beautiful life full of things I could never have imagined. Thank you for bringing Melaku into my life. And Cass, who I don't hate, no matter what you think. I love you so much. And I am so, so proud of you.

Graciela   Mommy.

Age 42

Raul, **Cass**, *and* **Melaku** *sit in formal wear, waiting for* **Graciela**.

Raul   I'm a great driver.

Cass   Of course you are. Laku, you got your mask?

Melaku *pulls out his mask.*

Raul   Better than my daughter.

Cass   That's not hard. But still, with the memory problems and Melaku in the car I / just . . .

Melaku   I don't mind.

Raul   I drove the roads of Arecibo for years. That's practically motocross.

Pause.

Raul   It's only an hour drive to Jersey. And traffic's so light these days.

Pause.

Raul   My car has more space.

Pause.

Raul   This is ageism.

Pause.

Raul   Fine.

Cass   Thank you, Raul. I appreciate it.

Raul   That's a good trick. The silence.

Cass   I learned it from Freud.

Graciela *walks in.*

Raul   Finally.

Graciela   I'm so sorry. The brief for the Gonzalez case, the senior partners hate it. We have to go back to square one.

Raul   What's a brief?

Cass   Like an essay for the court. What does square one entail?

Graciela   Twenty-four hours of chaos. I feel awful, but I can't go with you guys.

Raul   What?

Cass   How are you just figuring this out now?

Graciela   There was a miscommunication about – It doesn't matter. I'm so sorry, Dad. If we miss a filing deadline, my client will go to jail.

Melaku   You can work in the car.

Cass   He's right. It's all remote still anyway.

Graciela   You don't know how long Puerto Rican funerals take.

Cass   Then just come for the ceremony. You can sneak out before the reception.

Raul   She is not sneaking out of my sister's funeral.

Cass   A compromise is better than –

Raul   Your Tia Sofia changed your diapers. If someone cleaned your butthole, you go to their funeral.

Graciela   I can't have this argument. I have to get to work.

Raul   What is wrong with you?

Cass   Laku, can you go to your room for a minute?

Melaku   Mom.

Cass   Melaku, now.

Melaku *stomps out*.

Raul   At least your son knows how to do what he's told.

Graciela   Don't you fucking talk about my son.

Cass   Let's try to avoid escalating words.

Raul   What am I supposed to tell your cousins? That some client is more important than their mother?

Graciela   They shouldn't even be having an event this big.

Raul   It's outdoors. Everyone is vaccinated. The CDC guidelines –

Graciela   Are no guarantee.

Raul   *Mira*, you are going to this funeral if I have to carry you.

Graciela   I'm not five, Dad.

Raul   You're acting like it. If your mother was here –

Graciela   But she's not. Because she wouldn't get one goddamn surgery.

Cass   Gratzi! / We talked about this.

Raul   She made her choice, *mija*.

Graciela   And you let her. / If you had pushed Mom to keep fighting . . .

Cass   That's not what happened / Gratzi.

Raul   We are not discussing your mother. We are going to this funeral *si tu quieres o no.*

He grabs her and starts pulling her towards the door. **Graciela** *resists.*

Graciela   What are you – . . . Let go of me.

Cass   Raul, this / is completely –

Raul   *Vamanos. Cassandra, toma mis / llaves.*

Graciela   I can't. / I can't.

Cass   What?

Raul   Keys. / Take my damn keys.

Graciela   I can't. I can't. I can't. (*Screaming.*) I CAN'T.

They all freeze, stunned by the force of **Graciela***'s scream.*

Graciela   I can't go to another funeral. Jordan. Mom. This whole . . . Hundreds of thousands of people are dead and everything just . . . goes on. I can't do it anymore. I can't take any more sadness or fear or . . . I can't hear people talk about how God has a plan when, if there is a god, he's a vicious bastard scum-fucking piece of shit. I can't listen to people lie that life is anything more than constant pain until you die.

A long pause.

Raul   I miss her too.

Pause.

Raul   It's gonna be okay, *mija.*

Graciela   How? How do people live with this? How do I do live with this?

Pause.

Raul   I don't know.

Age 49

Melaku *sits on his bed.* **Graciela** *enters.*

Graciela   This seat taken?

She sits next to him. They sit together for a moment.

Graciela   How ya doing?

Melaku   Momma Cass told you?

Graciela   She showed me the letter from school. Said you wouldn't talk to her about it.

Melaku   Because I'm fine.

Graciela   I know that fine. That fine is not fine.

Pause.

Graciela   You can tell me anything. I promise I can handle it.

Melaku   You had a panic attack when my fish died.

Graciela   That's an urban legend.

Melaku   And Tia Sofia? You freak out about death.

Graciela   Everyone freaks out about death. I'm just honest about it.

Pause.

Graciela   She was in your grade, right? The girl who . . .

Pause.

Graciela   Did you know her well?

Pause.

Graciela   If you think the silent treatment will work on me, you are not as smart as your grades suggest.

Melaku   She was in my math class.

Graciela   And . . .?

Melaku   You wouldn't understand.

Graciela (*suddenly excited*)   Oh my God! Oh my God!

Melaku   What?

Graciela   You did it. You finally become a surly teenager. I was starting to lose hope.

Melaku   That's not funny.

Graciela   It's a little funny.

Melaku   It's not fucking funny!

A long pause.

Graciela   My best friend did it. Jordan.

Melaku   My godfather?

Graciela *nods.*

Melaku   You said he had a heart attack.

Graciela   Adults lie. Get used to it.

Slight pause.

Melaku   What was it like, when he . . .?

Graciela   It was one of the worst days of my life. And then afterwards. For months. Years. Everything reminded me of him. Of how much I had lost. How much the world had lost. It's why I freaked out when your fish died.

Melaku   I knew that wasn't an urban legend.

Graciela   Losing people is awful. And losing someone to themselves is . . . But if there's one thing I learned from all that pain, it's that you can't do it alone.

Pause.

Melaku   The teachers are being so stupid.

Graciela   Death does that to people.

Melaku   They removed her desk. From math class. They even rearranged the chairs to get rid of the gap, like she never existed at all.

Graciela   How does that make you feel?

Melaku   Seriously?

Graciela   Sorry.

A long pause.

Graciela   I want you to promise me something. If you ever decide to . . . You kill me first.

Melaku   What?

Graciela   I'm not living in a world without you. So, if you wanna go, you buy two bullets.

Melaku   I thought you were gonna say I should go to therapy or something.

Graciela   I'm sure Momma Cass already covered that. But depression, all that stuff, it messes with your mind. Tricks you into thinking nobody will care if you die, or that they'll even be happy. Which is bullshit. There is no me in me without the way I love you. So, if you start thinking nobody cares if you live or die, you come kill me. Because I really don't wanna die, but I would rather you pulverize me with a pickaxe before you ever hurt yourself.

Melaku   This is a weird conversation.

Graciela   You have a weird mother. Two, in fact. But I think we did a pretty good job so far.

Melaku   So far?

Graciela   You've got six more months at home. We could still fuck it up.

He smiles. They share a moment.

Melaku   She seemed so normal. She had friends. She was good at school. Or at least math. She was crazy good at math.

Graciela   Yeah?

Melaku   We'd play jeopardy. To study for tests, you know. Make it fun.

Graciela   Doesn't sound fun.

Melaku   She won so much people complained it was unfair. She got in early to MIT. She had everything and she just . . . It makes no sense.

Graciela   It never does.

Melaku   It should.

Graciela   Yeah. It really should.

Age 52

Cass *sits in a hospital bed, eyes closed.* **Graciela** *rushes into the hallway, looking everywhere. A* **Medical Resident** *wanders on and notices* **Graciela**.

Resident   Can I help you, ma'am?

Graciela   Melaku Ruiz.

Resident   Excuse me?

Graciela   Cassandra Altman and Melaku Ruiz. They would have come in an hour ago. Less. There was an accident. I don't know exactly . . . A car crash I think.

Resident   You'll have to check in at the front desk.

Graciela   Do you know where people's rooms are?

Resident   Of course, but –

Graciela   Cassandra Altman and Melaku Ruiz.

Resident   We can't have people roaming the hallways without visitor badges.

Graciela   Then tell me where they are and I'll stop roaming.

Resident   I understand your rush / but –

Graciela   I got a voicemail from some man I've never met saying . . . I need to see them. Then I'll get whatever stupid badge.

Resident   Why don't you come with me to the front desk and –

Graciela   Are you paid to fuck with people?

Resident   I'm a resident. I'm barely paid at all.

Graciela   Tell me where they are. Please.

Resident   The hospital has rules.

Graciela   If it were you in an accident. If your mom were terrified, trying not to think about what might have happened. Wouldn't you want someone to help her?

Resident   We just need to confirm that you are family and then we can –

Graciela *grabs the* **Resident** *and slams her up against a wall.*

Graciela   Either my family is here and I need to see them now, or they're not and I have nothing to lose, so I am going to ask again and if you don't tell me, I will remove your fucking eyes from your fucking skull with my fucking thumbs. Do you understand?

The **Resident** *nods.*

Graciela   Room number?

Resident   B37.

Graciela   Thank you. Now go report the crazy lady to security.

*The **Resident** runs off. **Graciela** enters **Cass**'s room.*

Graciela   Thank God.

*She rushes over and hugs **Cass**.*

Cass   Ow.

Graciela   Sorry. Sorry. Are you okay?

Cass   Just my arm. And my forehead. And my car. And my pride.

Graciela   Some guy called me. He said something about a car accident.

Cass   I gave the nice man your number. My new phone got smashed. Pshew. No more pretty phone.

Graciela   But you're okay.

Cass   Morphine solves everything.

Graciela   And Laku?

Cass   I took my eyes off the road. You shouldn't do that. I was just so happy he was home.

Graciela   Cass!

Cass   Why are you so yelly?

Graciela   Tell me Laku's okay!

Cass   He's fine.

Graciela   Fine? He's fine?

She breathes for the first time.

Cass   No broken nothing. I checked before I let them . . . with the morphine.

Graciela   Where is he?

Cass   Cafeteria. I don't think he eats enough at that school. We should send more care packages.

Graciela   So no one . . .

Cass   No one?

Graciela   No one died.

Cass   Just my new iPhone.

Age 61

Graciela *and* **Melaku** *stand in front of a table.* **Raul**'*s body lies on the table*.

Graciela   He looks so pale.
He hated not having a tan. I had to have the nurses remove the mirrors in his room. Couldn't remember his own name by the end but he knew he was "from island people" and island people are brown.
He'd try to talk to me in Spanish.
Forgot he never taught me. Forgot who I even was.
But he never forgot Arecibo.
I tried to bribe one of the nurses to leave him out in the yard for a few days. Build up a base coat. But they didn't want him getting skin cancer.
Cancer woulda been a fucking blessing compared to . . .
Don't tell Momma Cass I said that.
I thought it would be easier. Knowing ahead of time. Not suddenly . . .
But no, it's still agony.
I'm supposed to be an adult.
I'm a fucking grandma.
But I look at him and I feel like I'm five years old, screaming my head off that it's not fair he's gone.
I guess I don't scream out loud anymore.
Is that progress?

Pause.

Graciela   You have your mother's silence.

Melaku   It's gonna be okay.

Graciela   He always said that. 'It's gonna be okay, *mija*.'
Now he'll never say it again.

Pause.

Graciela   The last person who loved me is gone.

Melaku   I love you. And Momma Cass. And your friends.

Graciela   That's not the same. You love me because I took
care of you. They loved me just for existing. You'll see. You
won't know till you lose it. The hollowness. What it feels like
to know your parents will never hug you again.

Slight pause.

Graciela   I'm an orphan.

Lily *enters, mouth covered in chocolate.*

Lily   Daddy, you're taking for always.

Melaku   Come here, Lily Pad. You've got chocolate all over
your face.

Lily   Mommy said I could get ice cream if I was patient but
then you took forever and I'm tired of being sad and
Mommy yelled at me for trying to put Jenny in the Em-Rye.

Melaku   Why would you put the baby in an MRI?

Lily *shrugs.*

Lily   Jenny wanted to go to the moon.

Melaku   Would you like to say goodbye?

Graciela   Are you sure that's . . .

Melaku   Children are strong.

Lily *comes over and looks at the body. She understands, more or less.*

Lily   He looks nice.

Melaku   He was your great-grandpa.

Lily   That's good. My other grandpa is just okay.

They all look at the body. A long pause.

Lily   I want pizza.

Melaku   Why don't you go tell Mommy?

Lily *leaves.*

Melaku   We tried to explain that today was a serious day
but . . .

Graciela   She's perfect.

Melaku   I should make sure she doesn't climb into a bin of
used needles. I'll let you say goodbye to Abbo.

He exits. She stares at the body.

Graciela   Come back, Daddy. Please. I can't do this alone.

Age 64

Graciela *and* **Cass** *sit at their table.*

Graciela   We could have the hottest deck in Bed-Stuy.

Cass   And you could have another project to waste
money on.

Graciela   We'll have deck parties every week, the coolest
grannies on the block. Laku and Yasmine can take the train
in with Lily and Jenny. We'll invite Lisa and Raych. It'll be a
hootenanny.

Cass   You can't just declare things a hootenanny.

Graciela   I can once I have a deck.

Cass   Decks have hootenanny powers?

Graciela   The hootenaniest.

Graciela's *watch buzzes. She looks at it.*

Graciela   Holy shit. Frank died.

Cass   Frank from your firm? He's not that old.

Graciela   Sixty. Maybe younger. He had a heart attack.

Cass   Did you know he had heart problems?

Graciela   I mean, he stopped playing summer softball a couple years ago, but I just assumed that was because he sucked.

Cass   His poor wife.

Graciela   Unless she killed him.

Cass   Why would she kill him?

Graciela   That's a thing straight couples do. Like boogey boarding or mediocre sex.

Cass   I'm sure not all straight couples boogey board.

Pause.

Graciela   We're next.

Cass   What?

Graciela   People in our generation are starting to die of old age. It's just a matter of time.

Cass   Isn't it always just a matter of time?

Graciela   How can you be so calm?

Cass   People are born. People die. That's life.

Graciela   We'll see if you're so Zen when Laku and I are spoon-feeding you Jell-O on your deathbed.

Cass   Why do you assume you're gonna outlive me?

Graciela   You eat Velveeta cheese. Regularly.

Cass   It tastes like happiness.

Graciela   We're gonna die, Cass. We're gonna . . . We are going to die. We're gonna die.

Age 68

Graciela   Hey.

Cass   Should I go to AFTA this year? It's in Arizona.

Graciela   I think Hannah . . . I went next door to borrow her vacuum and there were thirty old Jews in suits looking sad.

Cass   Do you know how?

Graciela *shakes her head*.

Graciela   I hope she went out great. I hope she flipped her Corvette off a cliff.

Cass   She was eighty and drove a Honda.

Graciela   I hope she stole a Corvette and flipped it off a cliff.

Age 71

Graciela   Lisa said it was a stroke. Paramedics couldn't do anything.

Cass   That's awful.

Graciela   One minute you're planning summer on the Grove and the next you're gone.

Cass   How's Lisa taking it?

Graciela   Like her wife died.

Age 73

Cass   Bone cancer, I think, but it spread to her brain.

Age 75

Graciela   Heart attack.

Age 78

Cass   Diabetes.

Age 80

Graciela   Cancer.

Age 81

Cass   Alzheimer's.

Age 81

Graciela   Cancer.

Age 81

Cass   Flu.

Graciela   Flu?

Cass   Flu.

Age 82

Graciela   Stroke.

Age 84

Cass Seriously? I thought her cancer was in remission?

Graciela She got hit by a bus.

Pause.

Graciela At least it wasn't cancer.

Age 85

Graciela You said it would be fine!

Melaku I know.

Graciela Does she look fine?

Melaku I was wrong. I'm sorry, Eema.

Graciela Sorry won't bring her back to life. Sorry won't . . .

Melaku You need to calm down.

Graciela Calm down? How the hell am I supposed to calm down?

Melaku Because it's just a turtle.

Graciela Your granddaughter's turtle. She's gonna hate me forever.

Melaku She's three.

Graciela Kids hold grudges. Trust me.

Melaku Theresa loves you more than Mrs. Picklesworth.

Graciela Tell her it was you.

Melaku How would I have killed the turtle she left with you?

Graciela Hammer?

Melaku You want me to tell my granddaughter I beat Mrs. Picklesworth to death with a hammer?

Graciela Say it was self-defense.

Melaku All you had to do was feed her.

Graciela I did feed her!

Melaku *is not buying it.*

Graciela It's possible I may have forgotten to refill the water.

Melaku Seriously?

Graciela It's a reptile.

Melaku A marine reptile.

Graciela I have a busy life.

Melaku In a nursing home?

Graciela Senior living facility. We've got ping-pong tournaments, lectures, ballroom dancing.

Melaku So your excuse is you were too busy doing the tango with Momma Cass?

Graciela Not just your mother. All the women here want a lead who won't grope them.

Melaku There are so many things wrong with that, I'm just going to pretend you never said it.

Graciela How sharper than a serpent's tooth . . .

Melaku To have a thankless child. I know. I also know that line comes from a play about a crazy old asshole who disowns his child for telling the truth and ruins his life.

Pause.

Graciela I never should have taught you to read.

Melaku We all make mistakes.

Graciela Fine. You can tell her that her great-grandmother slaughtered her beloved pet.

Melaku   How reasonable.

Graciela   As long as you say that great-grandma was Cass.

Age 86

Graciela *sits in a hospital bed, surrounded by* **Melaku**, **Lily**, *and* **Cass**. *A* **Nurse** *walks in with a covered food tray.*

Nurse   Breakfast time, Mrs. Ruiz.

Graciela   Call me *mija*.

Nurse   I'm a little young for you to be my daughter.

Graciela   Are you saying I'm old?

Nurse   *Claro que no.*

Graciela   Sorry, I don't actually speak Spanish.

Nurse   Graciela Ruiz?

Graciela   My father wanted me to assimilate. You whippersnappers don't know how easy you have it.

Melaku   Since when do you call people whippersnappers?

Graciela   I'm trying out new hobbies.

She suddenly doubles over in pain.

Nurse   We're going to make you as comfortable as possible, Mrs. Ruiz.

Graciela   *Mija.*

Cass   Why do you want him to . . .?

Graciela   It just feels right.

Nurse   We're going to make you as comfortable as possible, *mija*. Hospice is about finding the most painless and respectful passing.

Graciela   Where's the drugs?

Nurse We have you on fentanyl. You can push that button by your hand to increase the dosage. We recommend being . . . judicious.

Graciela What's it gonna do, kill me?

Nurse It can make it hard for patients to be present.

Graciela I've been present for eighty-six years. If you give me a button to make life bearable, I'm pushing that shit.

Nurse Whatever you want.

Cass Thank you for being so patient.

The **Nurse** *gestures to the food tray.*

Nurse Try to eat. I got the cafeteria staff to make you a special breakfast.

He takes off the top of the bowl. **Graciela** *recognizes it instantly.*

Graciela Farina.

She looks at him. He looks back at her. He's not the **Nurse** *anymore. He is* **Raul**.

Nurse It's gonna be okay, *mija.*

He leaves. **Graciela** *pulls herself together, then offers her IV to the room.*

Graciela Who wants fentanyl?

She spasms with pain again. **Melaku** *runs to her side.*

Graciela I'm fine. Relax.

Lily Is there anything we can get you?

Graciela There is one thing, Lily Pad. Just before I go, I'd like you to say, 'Dying must be so hard.'

Lily Why?

Graciela So my last words can be, 'Dying is easy. Comedy is hard.'

Melaku   Eema.

Graciela   Don't 'Eema' me. As a wise woman once said, 'My death, my rules.' You'll get your turn.

Cass (*to* **Melaku** *and* **Lily**)   Will you give us a second?

Lily   Come on, Dad. Let's find Theresa so we have an excuse to get ice cream.

Melaku *goes up to* **Graciela** *and puts a hand on her shoulder.*

Melaku   I . . .

Graciela   I know.

She reaches up and holds his hand. They share a moment, then **Melaku** *and* **Lily** *exit.*

Graciela   This family's dedication to ice cream in the face of death is my greatest accomplishment.

Cass   All these years and you still can't feel your feelings without cracking jokes.

Graciela   A girl's gotta make an exit. Tell me you didn't forget your tuba.

Cass   I love you.

Pause.

Graciela   You know, I really fucked up this no death thing.

Cass *takes* **Graciela**'s *hand. After a moment,* **Graciela** *spasms with pain. She hits the button.*

Graciela   Ooh, that's the stuff.

Slight pause.

Graciela   Tell me a story.

Cass   About what?

Graciela   A dog.

Cass   There once was a dog.

Graciela   What kinda dog?

Cass   A . . . good dog. A golden retriever.

Graciela   That's a nice kind of dog.

Cass   And he was –

Graciela   He?

Cass   I can make my dog any gender I want. And this dog was a male dog. And he had a . . . tail. As dogs so often do. And he liked his tail.

Graciela   This story sucks.

Cass   Take more fentanyl. And the dog had a friend dog. A lady dog. But they were just friends because he wasn't attracted to lady dogs.

Graciela   That's good. I like gay dogs.

Cass   She was a terrier. And they would go on adventures together. They'd run through the woods, and swim in ponds and sniff other dogs' butts. They were best friends. But after awhile, the dog noticed his terrier friend slowing down. Her little legs scurried slower when she ran. She was always panting when they got out of the lake. Her butt sniffing, though, that was still top notch. Then, one day, after years of swims and forest runs, after thousands of sniffed butts, his terrier friend didn't come to meet him. The golden retriever was worried. He went looking for her, but she was nowhere to be found.

Graciela (*sleepy*)   Where'd she go?

Cass   The woods were empty. The pond was empty. All the nearby butts were unsniffed.

Graciela (*even more sleepy*)   Not the butts.

Cass   So he went to her house. He looked all around the yard, but there was no sign of her. Through the windows, he could see her human family. He couldn't understand them because he was a dog, but he saw everyone rushing around and shouting those weird human sounds. He scratched against the door, demanding to be let in. They were distracted, so he decided to use his friend's dog door. The terrier-sized door was too small for his golden retriever body, but this was an emergency. He shoved his big head through the little door and there he saw her, his best friend, lying on the ground, panting softly, surrounded by five tiny terrier puffballs. He was gonna be an uncle.

Graciela *is gone.* **Cass** *holds her hand.*

End of life.

End of play.

Printed in the USA
CPSIA information can be obtained
at www.ICGtesting.com
LVHW020936171024
794056LV00003B/788

9 781350 430099